PROPERTY OF
KATE GOODRICH LIBRARY
505 WEST TENTH STREET

UTAH JAZZ

by Brian Howell

Published by ABDO Publishing Company, 8000 West 78th Street, Edina, Minnesota 55439. Copyright © 2012 by Abdo Consulting Group, Inc. International copyrights reserved in all countries. No part of this book may be reproduced in any form without written permission from the publisher. SportsZone™ is a trademark and logo of ABDO Publishing Company.

Printed in the United States of America,
North Mankato, Minnesota
062011
092011

 THIS BOOK CONTAINS AT LEAST 10% RECYCLED MATERIALS.

Editor: Chrös McDougall
Copy Editor: Anna Comstock
Series design: Christa Schneider
Cover production: Kazuko Collins
Interior production: Carol Castro

Photo Credits: Colin E Braley/AP Images, cover; Douglas C. Pizac/AP Images, 1, 8, 47; Scott A. Miller/AP Images, 4; Jack Smith/AP Images, 7, 43 (bottom); Mark J. Terrill/AP Images, 11, 35, 42 (bottom); Jeff Haynes/AFP/Getty Images, 13, 43 (top); AP Images, 14, 42 (top), 19, 20; Charles Kelly/AP Images, 17; Greg Lehman/AP Images, 23; David Breslauer/AP Images, 24; Richard J. Carson/AP Images, 26; Mike Powell/Getty Images, 29; Jeff Kida/AP Images, 31, 42 (middle); David J. Phillip/AP Images, 32; Tom Olmscheid/AP Images, 36; Steve C. Wilson/AP Images, 39, 43 (middle); Jim Urquhart/AP Images, 41; Delcia Lopez/AP Images, 44

Library of Congress Cataloging-in-Publication Data
Howell, Brian, 1974-
  Utah Jazz / by Brian Howell.
    p. cm. -- (Inside the NBA)
  Includes index.
  ISBN 978-1-61783-177-5
  1. Utah Jazz (Basketball team)--History--Juvenile literature. I. Title.
  GV885.52.U8H68 2012
  796.323'6409792258--dc23
                                    2011020547

TABLE OF CONTENTS

Chapter 1 ....Stockton to Malone, 4

Chapter 2 ....Jazz in New Orleans, 14

Chapter 3 ....Moving West, 20

Chapter 4 ....Joining the Elite, 26

Chapter 5 ....A New Tune, 36

Timeline, 42

Quick Stats, 44

Quotes and Anecdotes, 45

Glossary, 46

For More Information, 47

Index, 48

About the Author, 48

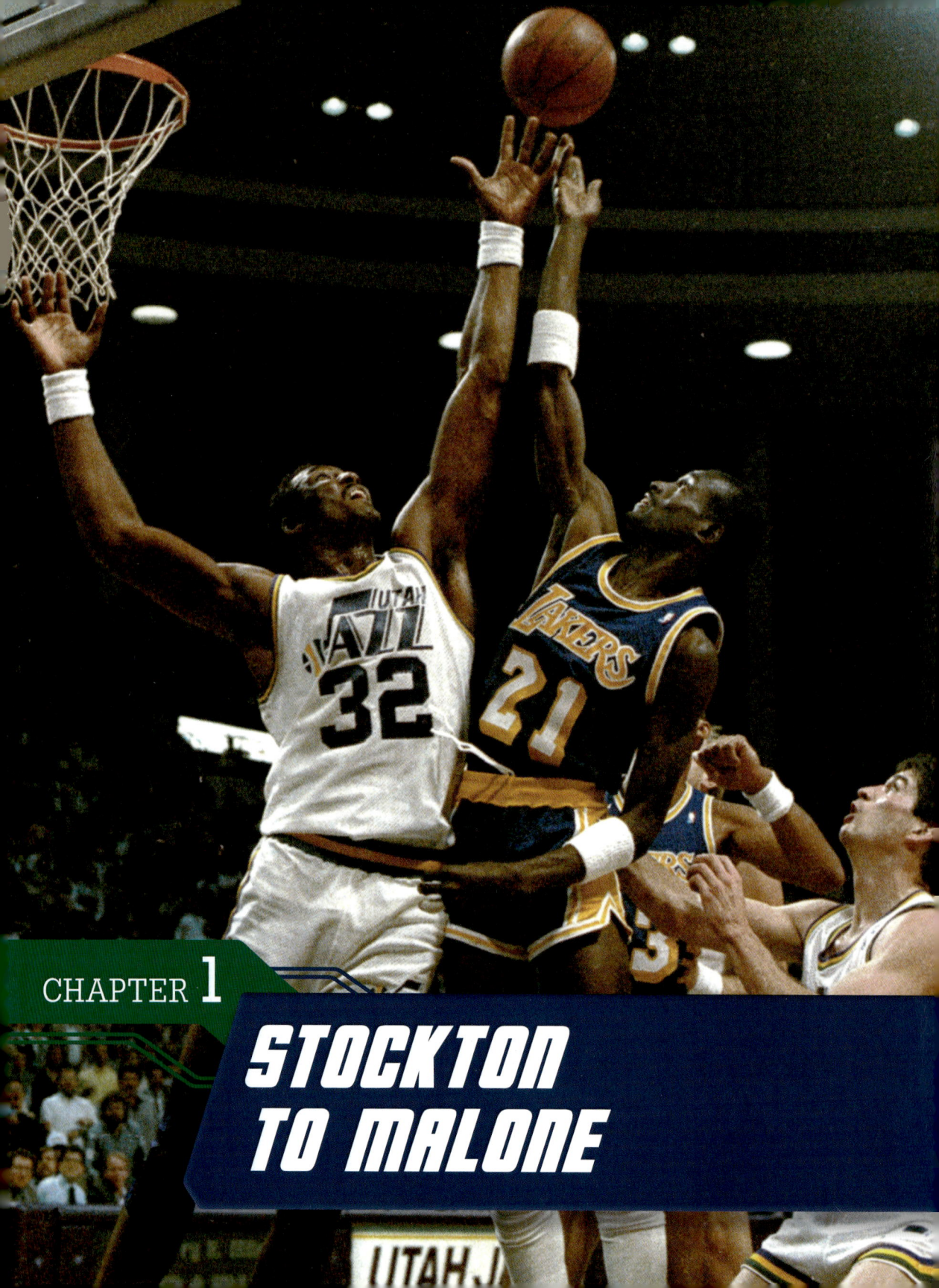

CHAPTER 1

STOCKTON TO MALONE

"**S**tockton to Malone . . . it's good!" National Basketball Association (NBA) broadcasters got used to saying that phrase during John Stockton and Karl Malone's 18 years together on the Utah Jazz. Together, they led the team to its best seasons.

Stockton joined the Jazz as a first-round draft pick in 1984. Malone came on as a first-round draft pick one year later. The Jazz made the playoffs during all 18 seasons that both Stockton and Malone were on the team.

Individually, the two were great players. Stockton was a 6-foot-1 point guard with a pass-first mentality that was unmatched by most players. In 2009, he was inducted into the Naismith Memorial Basketball Hall of Fame. Stockton finished his remarkable career with more steals (3,265) and assists (15,806) than any player

Jazz power forward Karl Malone (32) goes for a rebound while point guard John Stockton, right, watches during a 1987 game.

AWESOME DUO

John Stockton and Karl Malone came from very different backgrounds. Stockton grew up in Spokane, Washington, and stayed there to play his college ball at Gonzaga University. Malone, on the other hand, grew up across the country in Louisiana and starred at Louisiana Tech University. But the two had instant chemistry on the court when they became teammates in the NBA. It worked wonders for nearly two decades.

During their 18 years together, a countless number of Malone's points came from Stockton's assists. With Hall of Famer Jerry Sloan as their coach, Stockton and Malone made the pick-and-roll a lethal part of their game. A pick-and-roll is a designed play where one player sets a pick for another. Then, he rolls to an open spot on the floor and looks for a pass from the other player so he can score a basket.

in professional basketball history.

There was nothing flashy about Stockton's game. He just simply got the job done. "He's the best," former NBA star point guard Gary Payton once said. "When I came into the league, he was the guy who took me to school. I'm still looking for a weakness in his game."

Malone was a 6-foot-9 power forward who could score and rebound like few other players in NBA history. He joined Stockton in the Hall of Fame in 2010. Malone retired as the second-leading scorer in league history, with 36,928 total points. And through 2010–11, only five players in history have grabbed more rebounds than his 14,968. Malone was also named the NBA's Most Valuable Player (MVP) twice.

Coach Jerry Sloan was the third cornerstone, along with John Stockton and Karl Malone, during the Jazz's run of success in the 1990s.

While Stockton beat opponents with tremendous fundamentals, Malone overpowered his opponents with physical strength. He carried a muscular 250 pounds on his large frame. "He runs the court like a small man, then overpowers bigger people," longtime

All-Time Greats

In 1996, the NBA named its 50 greatest players of all time. Karl Malone and John Stockton were both included on that list. Malone and Stockton were also members of the Dream Team. That was the nickname for the 1992 US men's basketball team that won an Olympic gold medal in Barcelona, Spain.

Sharing the Moment

Karl Malone and John Stockton combined for 24 All-Star Game appearances. The 1993 game was one of their best. Played in front of their home fans in Salt Lake City, Utah, Malone and Stockton both starred in helping the Western Conference team win. At the end of the game, they were named co-MVPs. "If you wrote a movie, that's how it would end," Malone said.

NBA coach Don Nelson said early in Malone's career. "Is there a more dominant power forward in the game today? If there is, I'd like to see him."

Stockton and Malone were the Jazz's superstars from the mid-1980s through the early 2000s. Coach Jerry Sloan was the other standard for the Jazz during those years. The respected coach was at the helm from the start of the 1988–89 season until midway through the 2010–11 season. With those three cornerstones in place, the Jazz reached their peak during the 1996–97 and 1997–98 NBA seasons.

Although he was getting older, Malone had one of his best seasons in 1996–97. The 33-year-old was voted as the NBA's MVP that season after averaging 27.4 points, 9.9 rebounds, and 4.5 assists per game. Stockton was brilliant, too. And shooting guard Jeff Hornacek provided Utah a great spark on offense. Two newcomers to the starting lineup—26-year-old forward Bryon Russell and 23-year-old center Greg Ostertag—performed well, too. That group, coached by Sloan, took the Jazz to a place they had never been before: the NBA Finals.

NBA MVP Karl Malone goes for a basket during Game 5 of the 1997 Finals. He averaged 27.4 points, 9.9 rebounds, and 4.5 assists per game that season.

Waiting for the Jazz in the Finals were the defending NBA champion Chicago Bulls. Led by superstar Michael Jordan, the Bulls had dominated that season and breezed through the playoffs.

But Utah gave the Bulls fits in the Finals. The series was tied at two games each after Game 4. In Game 5, the Bulls needed a heroic effort from Jordan, including a big three-pointer in the closing seconds, to beat the Jazz 90–88. Then in Game 6, Utah had the game tied at 86–86 in the final seconds before the Bulls scored the final four points to win 90–86. In the end, the Bulls won the championship four games to two.

"We played our hearts out and just came up a little bit short," Sloan said.

Utah was not finished, though. The Jazz won 62 games and another Midwest Division championship the next season. After taking out the Houston Rockets in the first round of the playoffs, the Jazz breezed through the San Antonio Spurs and the Los Angeles Lakers in the following rounds to get back to the NBA Finals.

Once again, Jordan and the Bulls were waiting. The Bulls of the late-1990s were one of the most dominant teams in NBA history. Behind Jordan and teammate Scottie Pippen, the Bulls had won five NBA championships between 1991 and 1997. Many favored them to win their sixth—and third in a row—in 1997–98. However, others were sick of the Bulls. They wanted to see Stockton, Malone, Sloan, and the Jazz take home the franchise's first NBA title.

The 1998 Finals were just as close as the 1997 Finals. The

Jazz guard Jeff Hornacek, *right*, guards Chicago Bulls superstar Michael Jordan during Game 2 of the 1998 NBA Finals.

Jazz opened the series with an 88–85 overtime victory at home in the Delta Center. Stockton led the Jazz with 24 points, including seven in overtime. But the Jazz had come into the series with much more time off than the Bulls. Two days later, a better-rested Bulls squad won 93–88. Chicago then took the next two games at home, including a 96–54 drubbing in Game 3. That was the largest loss in NBA Finals history.

But the Jazz still had more fight in them. With the series on the line, Malone scored 39 points and grabbed nine rebounds to lead Utah to an 83–81 win. Then, back in Utah for Game 6, the Jazz held an 86–85 lead in the final seconds. It appeared that the series would go to a decisive Game 7. But it was not to be. In the final seconds of what many figured would be his final game ever, Jordan drained a remarkable jumper to give the Bulls their sixth title in eight years.

"We've been close the last two years," Hornacek said. "We want to come back and take one more chance at it."

Unfortunately for the Jazz, that was the closest they would come to an NBA championship through the 2010–11 season. Hornacek played two more years. Stockton and Malone played five more together. Although Malone was the NBA MVP again in 1998–99, the group never got back to the NBA Finals. In fact, they never even got back to the Western Conference finals.

Since the franchise began in New Orleans, Louisiana, the Jazz never has won a championship through the 2010–11 season. The 1997 and 1998 Jazz teams provided some great moments for their fans, though.

> **Friends for Life**
>
> The chemistry between John Stockton and Karl Malone was not limited to the basketball court. The two became close friends over the years. "He is like one of my older brothers to me, and not because he gives me the ball on the break," Malone once said. "Mess with Stockton and you mess with me." Stockton felt the same way. "He's a great friend of mine," Stockton said in 2003 after he retired. "And I'm thankful we were part of each other's families."

Jazz point guard John Stockton drives past a Chicago Bulls defender during the 1998 NBA Finals.

CHAPTER 2

JAZZ IN NEW ORLEANS

In March 1974, the NBA decided to expand. The 17-team league picked New Orleans, Louisiana, to be the home of the 18th team.

Sam Battistone and Fred Rosenfeld led a nine-man group that paid $6.15 million for the franchise. After a contest to name the team, the owners decided to call it the Jazz. The team name and logo were selected to honor the rich tradition of jazz music in New Orleans. The logo featured the "J" from Jazz as a musical note. And the team colors—purple, gold, and green—were selected to signify the importance of Mardi Gras to the city.

"Jazz is one of those things for which New Orleans is nationally famous and locally proud," Rosenfeld said. "It is a great art form which belongs to New Orleans and its rich history. As for the tradition of Mardi Gras, the three colors are emblematic: purple for

Jazz guard "Pistol Pete" Maravich drives for the hoop during a 1979 game. He was the team's first player.

PISTOL PETE

Pete Maravich was an All-Star and a Hall of Fame NBA player. He also might have been the best college player ever. At Louisiana State University, where his father was the coach, "Pistol Pete" averaged an astonishing 44.2 points per game. He was known for his great showmanship on the court.

The Atlanta Hawks selected the 6-foot-5 guard with the third pick in the 1970 NBA Draft. He struggled to fit in with the Hawks, though. Many of his older teammates did not like his style—or his big contract. Still, Maravich was a standout player when the Jazz traded for him in 1974. He reached his peak with the Jazz, making the All-Star game three times in five years and leading the league with 31.1 points per game in 1976–77. The Jazz waived Maravich in 1980. In 1988, at the age of 40, he died after suffering a heart attack while playing a pick-up basketball game.

justice, green for faith, gold for power."

The first player in Jazz team history was guard "Pistol Pete" Maravich. He had starred at Louisiana State University, which is located about 80 miles (129 km) from New Orleans, until 1970. He was then drafted by the Atlanta Hawks and became an All-Star. The Jazz traded for Maravich on May 3, 1974.

Maravich was not only the first player in team history; he also quickly became the Jazz's first star. In 5 1/2 seasons with the team, Maravich averaged 25.2 points per game. He was also the first Jazz player to be named to the All-NBA first team. In fact, he had that honor in 1975–76 and 1976–77.

The 6-foot-5 Maravich did not lack in confidence. "When I'm on, nobody can stop me,"

The Jazz's Pete Maravich cuts through three Atlanta Hawks defenders during a 1975 game in Atlanta.

he said. "I can do anything on the court I want."

Maravich proved that with a great season in 1974–75. He scored 21.5 points per game in the Jazz's first season. But as a team, the Jazz struggled. They won just six of their first 50 games. Coach Scotty Robertson was let go after the Jazz started 1–14. Under new coach Bill Van Breda Kolff, the Jazz played better down the stretch, winning 17 of their last 32.

The Jazz played at Municipal Auditorium and Loyola Field House during that first season. Before their second season, the Louisiana Superdome opened in New Orleans. The Superdome was built at a cost of more than $160 million. It was built for the New Orleans Saints of the National Football League, the Tulane University football team, and the Jazz.

The Jazz got off to a great start in the Superdome. They

> ### Trucking Along
>
> Len "Truck" Robinson produced one of the greatest single-season performances in Jazz history. He joined the Jazz for the 1977–78 season, during which he averaged 22.7 points and a career-high 15.7 rebounds per game. He was named to the All-NBA first team for his efforts. The next season, Robinson was averaging 24.2 points and 13.4 rebounds per game when the Jazz traded him to the Phoenix Suns.

won their first five games in their new home. On November 5, 1975, the Jazz defeated the Los Angeles Lakers 113–110 in front of 26,511 fans. At the time, that was the NBA record for attendance at a game. And that win gave the Jazz an NBA-best record of 6–1.

Center Otto Moore knew it was too early to celebrate, though. "I don't do any extra jumping up or down or get excited," he said. "I remember one year in Detroit we started out 13–1. In a few weeks, we were 13–10."

Sure enough, after that win the Jazz lost six in a row and 15 of their next 17 games. They finished with another losing record that season. One bright spot, however, was Maravich. The future Hall of Fame player averaged 25.6 points per game during that second season.

The Jazz tried to get Maravich some help in 1976 when they traded for guard Gail Goodrich, who was a five-time All-Star. Like Maravich, Goodrich was also one of the NBA's top scorers.

"He's a great shooter and I'm going to get the ball to him," Maravich said. "He's also going to make me better. When he's on, he's going to be double-teamed, and that will leave me open."

Unfortunately for the Jazz, Goodrich missed most of that

Jazz guard Gail Goodrich drives around Buffalo Braves defender Marvin Barnes during a 1978 game.

first year with an injury. In all, he played only three seasons with the Jazz. As promised, though, Goodrich and Maravich were a tough duo to stop.

But as good as Maravich and Goodrich were, the Jazz struggled with them on the roster. The first five seasons of Jazz history provided great moments here and there. But the Jazz never got to the playoffs or posted a winning record during that time. After a few seasons they also struggled to attract fans and make money.

So at the end of their fifth season, the Jazz moved to Salt Lake City, Utah.

JAZZ IN NEW ORLEANS **19**

CHAPTER 3

MOVING WEST

The Jazz had spent five seasons in New Orleans. Jazz co-owner Sam Battistone said the owners did not want to move, but they could no longer make it work in New Orleans. So the owners moved the team to Salt Lake City during the summer of 1979.

"We feel very strongly that the city of Salt Lake and the state of Utah can support the team," he said. NBA commissioner Lawrence O'Brien agreed. "Salt Lake is a hotbed of interest for basketball," he said.

Utah had a brief history of professional basketball. In 1970, the Los Angeles Stars of the American Basketball Association (ABA) moved to Utah and became the Utah Stars. The Stars had great success. They won the ABA championship in

Jazz guard Darrell Griffith rises in the air for a flying hook shot during a 1981 game against the Indiana Pacers.

MOVING WEST

> ### End of an Era
>
> On January 17, 1980, the Jazz said good-bye to their first player and first star, Pete Maravich. Coming back from a serious knee injury, Maravich played in just 17 games for Utah in 1979–80. Although Maravich was only 32 years old, he was not the same player after the injury. Since the Jazz were trying to rebuild their roster, they decided they needed to move on without Maravich. After being released by Utah, Maravich signed with the Boston Celtics. He finished out the season in Boston and then retired. The Jazz later retired his No. 7 jersey.

1971, finished as runner-up in 1974, and won three division titles in five years.

Although they had great fan support at the Salt Palace, the Stars folded during the 1975–76 season. At the end of that season, the ABA folded too, although four ABA teams joined the NBA. The league featured many great players, but it did not have as much national popularity as the NBA.

With the Jazz moving west, professional basketball finally returned to Salt Lake City. However, the change of scenery did not help the Jazz. After five losing seasons in New Orleans, the Jazz continued their losing ways in Utah.

During each of their first four seasons in Utah, the Jazz finished at or near the bottom of the Midwest Division. But while the losing continued, the Utah Jazz were building a stronger team.

The Jazz had hired Frank Layden as general manager upon moving to Utah. He spent the first several seasons overhauling the team's roster. Layden added key players in Allan Bristow and Ron Boone. He also traded for forward/guard Adrian Dantley, who became Utah's next great star.

Dantley had a strange beginning to his NBA career.

Emerging Jazz star guard Darrell Griffith throws down a dunk for two of his 28 points during a 1983 win over the Seattle SuperSonics.

He was the NBA's Rookie of the Year with the Buffalo Braves, but was traded to the Indiana Pacers after the season. Early in his second season, he was the NBA's second-leading scorer while playing for the Pacers. But he played only 23 games with Indiana before being traded to the Los Angeles Lakers. Then, after being one of the Lakers' best players for a year and a half, he was traded to the Jazz before the 1979–80 season.

"He's a great player and we worked hard to get him," Layden said. "Three other teams made serious mistakes about him."

Layden's focus was on building a team full of winners. Dantley was the type of player

MOVING WEST **23**

The Jazz's Rickey Green leaps into the air as he sets up a shot during a 1982 game against the Dallas Mavericks.

Dantley's Brilliance

In seven seasons with the Jazz, Adrian Dantley made the All-Star team six times. In four of those seasons, he averaged more than 30 points per game. The top player during Utah's first winning season, 1983–84, Dantley's jersey No. 4 was retired by the team in 2007. Dantley was inducted into the Hall of Fame in 2008.

he wanted. "Right after he got to Salt Lake City a rumor went around that we were thinking of trading him, so I went to Adrian and told him there's no way we'd trade him," Layden said. "We want Adrian Dantley to finish his career here."

Layden kept his promise—at least for a while. Dantley was traded to the Detroit Pistons in 1986. But before that, he played seven seasons with the Jazz and became one of the greatest players in team history.

Dantley averaged 28 points per game during his first season with the Jazz. He scored more than 30 points per game in each of the four years after that.

Even with Dantley, however, success did not come right away for the Jazz. They struggled for four years. But amid the struggles, the Jazz built the foundation for a successful future.

Layden fired coach Tom Nissalke and took over as coach 20 games into the 1981–82 season. But he kept the title of general manager, which meant that in addition to coaching the team, he also built the roster.

Over time, Layden and the Jazz added winning pieces to the puzzle. They drafted guard Darrell Griffith and signed point guard Rickey Green in 1980. In 1982, they acquired talented veteran forward John Drew in a trade, and they took Mark Eaton, a 7-foot-4 center, in the draft. The next year, the Jazz took forward Thurl Bailey in the 1983 draft.

The first nine years of Jazz history were filled with a lot of losses and a lot of change. But as the Jazz prepared for the 1983–84 season, they believed that the pieces they had in place would finally create a winning formula.

A Bad Deal

The Jazz used the third overall pick in the 1982 NBA Draft to select University of Georgia star Dominique Wilkins. But before Wilkins ever suited up for them, the Jazz traded him to the Atlanta Hawks for John Drew, Freeman Williams, and cash. Drew played only 2 1/2 seasons in Utah before being suspended for life by the NBA due to violating the league's substance abuse policy. And Williams played just 18 games in Utah before being released. Wilkins, meanwhile, was a nine-time All-Star during his 15-year career. As of 2011, he was the 11th-highest scorer in NBA history.

CHAPTER 4

JOINING THE ELITE

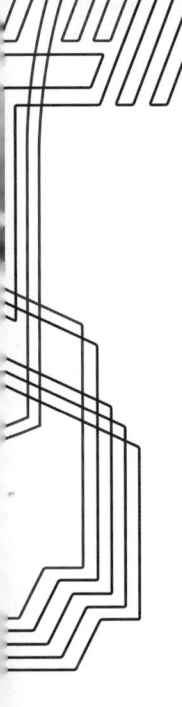

Considering the Jazz had never posted a winning record, most people had low expectations for the team going into the 1983–84 season. It was evident early in the season, however, that Utah was finally a good team.

"Before the season, many people had serious doubts about our players," coach Frank Layden said after his team improved to 22–12. "Now we've shown that we're a much better team than we were given credit for, and everyone's getting his just desserts. People

Golden Griff

On December 4, 1993, Darrell Griffith became the second player in Jazz history to have his jersey—No. 35—retired by the club. He is the only player in team history to be named NBA Rookie of the Year, which occurred in 1980–81. Griffith played his entire 10-year professional career in Utah, averaging 16.2 points per game.

Jazz forward Adrian Dantley goes up for a contested layup during a 1985 playoff game against the Houston Rockets.

JOINING THE ELITE **27**

finally have to seriously ask things like, 'Isn't Rickey Green one of the best point guards in the league?'"

The answer to that was, "Yes." Green did play like one of the best point guards in the league. Adrian Dantley and Darrell Griffith played like All-Stars, too. In addition to those three, John Drew was one of the best reserves in the league, Mark Eaton was one of the best defensive centers in the league, and Thurl Bailey was one of the best rookies in the league.

With talent like that, Utah finally put a winning product on the floor. In 1983–84, the Jazz had a lot of firsts. They had their first winning season, going 45–37. They won their first division championship. They made the playoffs for the first time ever. And they even won a playoff series for the first time, knocking out the Denver Nuggets in the first round. The Jazz finally fell to the Phoenix Suns in the playoffs' second round. After that remarkable season, Layden was named the NBA's Coach of the Year.

"I'm very proud and very happy for this team," Layden said. "They have been criticized, but they have played well this season."

The 1983–84 season was the start of a new standard of success for the Utah Jazz. After so many years of losing, the Jazz

> **Tall Order**
>
> From 1982 to 1993, 7-foot-4 center Mark Eaton was penciled into the starting lineup almost every game. A great defensive player, Eaton was 25 years old when he finished college and entered the NBA. He was older than most rookies because after high school, he went to a trade school and worked at a tire store for three years. Eventually, however, he was talked into enrolling in college and again playing basketball.

Jazz center Mark Eaton, *left*, and Los Angeles Lakers big man Kareem Abdul-Jabbar take a break during a 1988 game.

finally learned how to win. And once they learned how to win, they did not forget. That season was the first of 20 straight playoff seasons for the Jazz. In 27 seasons from 1983–84 to 2009–10, Utah made the playoffs 24 times and had a .500 record or better 26 times.

Layden led Utah to its first five playoff appearances. He got the Jazz to the second round three of those times. It was an especially impressive feat considering the Jazz lost a couple of their best players during that time.

Dantley, who was one of the first greats in team history, helped the Jazz reach the playoffs three times. Following the 1985–86 season, however,

JOINING THE ELITE **29**

he was traded to the Detroit Pistons. The star player and coach Layden did not get along. In return, the Jazz got Kelly Tripucka. He had made two All-Star teams and averaged more than 20 points per game in five seasons with Detroit. Tripucka never matched that production in two years with the Jazz, though.

The Jazz also lost Drew. A valuable scorer off the bench, Drew gave the Jazz a lift for two years. But his career ended early in the 1984–85 season. The NBA suspended Drew for life because of his repeated problems with substance abuse.

While the Jazz lost Dantley and Drew, they also added two other important players. In the first round of the 1984 NBA Draft, Utah selected point guard John Stockton from Gonzaga University. The next year, the Jazz drafted Louisiana Tech power forward Karl Malone.

Adding those two youngsters proved to be monumental for the Jazz. During his first three years in the NBA, Stockton was a backup to Green. The two of them formed a tremendous duo at point guard. Malone stepped into the starting lineup as a rookie and quickly established himself as a strong player.

In the 1987–88 season, Malone, Stockton, and Bailey— all under the age of 27—led the Jazz. They had all established themselves as individual

Key Contributor

Thurl Bailey never won any NBA awards or earned a trip to an All-Star Game. But he was an unsung hero for the Jazz. He played parts of 10 seasons in Utah, mostly coming off the bench. He averaged 14 points and 5.5 rebounds per game for the Jazz. And twice he posted more than 19 points per game.

The Jazz's Karl Malone defends against the Phoenix Suns' Tom Chambers during a 1990 playoff game.

stars, but they also played well together. Teaming the youngsters with veterans such as guard Griffith, center Eaton, and guard Green, Utah won 47 games. The Jazz also advanced to the second round of the playoffs.

The future looked bright for Utah and Layden. But despite all the success the Jazz had on the court, Layden was worn out. Just 17 games into the 1988–89 season, he quit as coach and general manager, taking a new position as team president.

"The game totally consumes you," said Layden, who was 56 years old at the time. "You are no longer in charge of your life."

Jazz point guard John Stockton fires a pass as he dives between two Houston Rockets defenders during the 1994 Western Conference finals.

One of the reasons Layden quit was that he was tired of the verbal abuse he took from fans. His decision to leave surprised the team. "Frank is one of the greatest coaches and motivators in the game, and he just hangs it up," Malone said. "I already miss him. I dedicate the rest of my career to him."

While players were sad to see Layden go, his replacement was ready to take charge. Jazz assistant coach Jerry Sloan was appointed as the new head coach. "You're not going to find a guy who works harder than Jerry Sloan," Layden said.

Sloan showed his work ethic during his Hall of Fame

coaching career. Before retiring midway through the 2010–11 season, Sloan led the Jazz to 19 playoff appearances in 22 seasons. He won more than 1,100 games as the team's head coach.

Led mainly by Malone and Stockton, and guided by coach Sloan, the Jazz became one of the NBA's best teams. In 1992, 1994, and 1996, the Jazz reached the Western Conference finals.

As the 1996–97 NBA season got underway, many considered Utah to be a good team, but not great. *Sports Illustrated* picked them to finish third in the Midwest Division, behind the San Antonio Spurs and the Houston Rockets.

Malone and Stockton were getting older. Both were in their mid-30s that season. And another key player, Jeff Hornacek, turned 34 that postseason. Although the Jazz had

Quite a Shot

Throughout his NBA career, shooting guard Jeff Hornacek was one of the best shooters in the league. In 14 seasons, he made 49.6 percent of his shots and scored 14.5 points per game. With the Jazz from 1994 to 2000, Hornacek was an important part of the offense. He helped lead Utah to seven straight playoff appearances. In 2002, the Jazz retired his No. 14 jersey.

been to the Western Conference finals three times in the previous five seasons, some did not think they had it in them to make another deep playoff run.

Houston, as many figured, was very good. The Rockets won 57 games that season. San Antonio, on the other hand, lost star player David Robinson to a season-ending injury six games into the season. The Spurs won just 20 games. The Jazz turned out to be much better than what some figured. Behind Malone's MVP season, the Jazz had the best record in the Western Conference at 64–18. Then they marched back to the Western Conference finals, losing only one game in the process.

To get to their first Finals, the Jazz had to beat the strong Rockets team. Utah got off to a good start, taking a two-games-to-one lead. But the Rockets came back to win Game 4.

The Jazz took a 3–2 lead by winning Game 5. Then, in Game 6, the Jazz trailed by seven points in the closing minutes. But they battled back to tie the game. Then, Stockton drained a game-winning three-pointer at the buzzer. Utah won the game, 103–100. They were headed for the NBA Finals, where they would face the Chicago Bulls.

"I took the shot and it felt good," Stockton said after the game. "I don't know how to explain it; it just felt good."

"They're no fluke; they're the real deal," Rockets coach Rudy Tomjanovich said. "They have a chance to win the championship, and I'll root for those guys in the finals."

Unfortunately for the Jazz, Michael Jordan and the Bulls were no fluke either. They beat the Jazz four games to two in the Finals. Utah had another chance in 1997–98, but Jordan and the Bulls again dispatched them in the NBA Finals. There was hope that the Jazz could take the next step in 1998–99, but it was not to be. Soon, a new generation of Jazz players would have to try to win the team its first NBA championship.

Karl Malone of the Jazz dunks the ball over a Chicago Bulls defender during Game 2 of the 1998 NBA Finals.

JOINING THE ELITE

CHAPTER 5

A NEW TUNE

Following the 2002–03 season, the Utah Jazz went through some drastic changes. Future Hall of Fame point guard John Stockton retired and future Hall of Fame power forward Karl Malone signed with the often-dominant Los Angeles Lakers in search of an NBA title. He played just one season with the Lakers—and failed to win a title—before retiring.

For the first time in nearly two decades, the Jazz did not have Stockton and Malone leading the way. It was also the first time in years that the Jazz had to deal with low expectations. Few people thought the Jazz would be able to get to the playoffs for a 21st straight season. Utah's playoff streak did end, but barely. The Jazz finished 42–40. That was just one game behind the Denver Nuggets, who clinched the final playoff spot in the Western Conference.

John Stockton, *bottom*, secures the ball while Karl Malone, *top*, looks on during a 2003 game against the Minnesota Timberwolves. The 2002–03 season was Stockton and Malone's last with the Jazz.

A NEW TUNE 37

> ### The Stopper
>
> Although the Jazz missed the play-offs three years in a row, from 2004 to 2006, forward Andrei Kirilenko made a name for himself as one of the league's best defensive players. He made the NBA's All-Defensive first team in 2005–06 after two years making the second team. He made the All-Star team in 2004. And in 2005–06, Kirilenko led the NBA with 220 blocks.

There was no Stockton or Malone, but the Jazz still had Jerry Sloan as a coach. And he did as much as he could with the new players Utah had.

"The fun part of coming to work every day for me is finding a way to win with the guys we have," Sloan said. "Physically we may be over-matched, but you can still play basketball if you do it as a group."

Utah took its expected dive the next year, winning just 26 games. Then in 2005–06, the Jazz missed the playoffs for the third straight year, going 41–41. During those seasons, the Jazz were building for the future.

Forward Andrei Kirilenko had been a role player during Stockton and Malone's last two years together. He developed into a team leader when the legends retired. In addition, the Jazz signed free agent big men Carlos Boozer and Mehmet Okur in 2004. They gave the Jazz some much-needed muscle near the basket.

The next year, the Jazz drafted point guard Deron Williams with the third pick in the 2005 draft. He might have been the most important player the Jazz added during the post-Stockton-and-Malone era.

During Williams's rookie season in 2005–06, the Jazz won 15 more games than they had the previous year. The next year, he helped Utah win 51

Teammates Carlos Boozer, *left*, and Andrei Kirilenko gave the Jazz a strong inside presence together from 2004 to 2010.

games and return to the playoffs for the first time in four years. The Jazz did not just get to the playoffs, though. They made it all the way to the conference finals before losing to the San Antonio Spurs.

Through the 2009–10 season, the Jazz never posted a losing record with Williams. They made the playoffs four

Shades of Malone

When the Jazz signed Carlos Boozer in 2004, they knew they were getting one of the best power forwards in the NBA—much like Karl Malone had been for nearly two decades in Utah. Boozer played six seasons for the Jazz, from 2004 to 2010. Although he missed a lot of games due to injuries, he was a dominant player when he was healthy. He made the All-Star team two times with Utah, in 2007 and 2008. In the summer of 2010, he signed with the Chicago Bulls.

SLOAN'S HISTORY

In 2010–11, Jerry Sloan began his 23rd season as the head coach of the Utah Jazz. And it would be his last. Sloan stepped down midway through the season, saying he had lost the energy to coach. Through 2010–11, his 1,221 career wins were third all time among NBA coaches.

Sloan spent more than 45 years in the NBA. He was an original member of the Chicago Bulls and played 10 seasons with them. He made two All-Star teams and later became the first player in team history to have his jersey number retired. Sloan later became a scout, assistant coach, and then head coach of the Bulls. In 1983, the Jazz hired him as a scout. He then worked four years as an assistant coach with the Jazz before becoming their head coach on December 9, 1988. When Sloan retired, the next longest-serving coach was the San Antonio Spurs' Gregg Popovich, who was hired December 10, 1996.

years in a row, from 2007 to 2010. Williams had finished second or third in the league in assists every year from 2007 to 2010, and he made his first All-Star game in 2010.

The optimism among Jazz fans abruptly faded during 2010–11, though. Boozer had left as a free agent before that season. Then on February 10, Sloan stepped down as coach after 23 seasons. He had been the longest-serving NBA coach by far at the time. Yet another devastating blow followed. On February 23, the Jazz traded Williams to the New Jersey Nets.

Suddenly, the once-promising team was starting over. The Jazz received talented young forward Derrick Favors, point guard Devin Harris, and a first-round pick in the Williams trade. They combined with forwards Al Jefferson,

Forward Paul Millsap is one of the players the Jazz are counting on to bring them back into contention in the Western Conference.

Kirilenko, and Paul Millsap to form the foundation of the new-look Jazz. However, Utah missed the playoffs for the first time since 2005–06.

After a rocky start to franchise history, the Jazz built a winning tradition behind Sloan, Stockton, and Malone. The team then rebuilt that tradition behind Sloan, Kirilenko, and Williams. But Jazz fans are hoping the next generation can finally lead the team to the one thing that has eluded it—the NBA title.

TIMELINE

1974	The New Orleans Jazz become the 18th team in the NBA.
1979	After five years in New Orleans, the Jazz move to Salt Lake City.
1984	In their tenth season, the Jazz finally reach the NBA playoffs for the first time.
1984	With the 16th pick in the NBA Draft, the Jazz select point guard John Stockton from Gonzaga University.
1985	Picking 13th in the NBA Draft, the Jazz select power forward Karl Malone from Louisiana Tech University.
1987	"Pistol" Pete Maravich, the first player and first star in Jazz history, is inducted into the Naismith Memorial Basketball Hall of Fame.
1988	Frank Layden, who led the Jazz to their first five playoff appearances, resigns as coach. Assistant coach Jerry Sloan replaces him.
1992	The Jazz reach the Western Conference finals for the first time in team history. They would also get there in 1994 and 1996.
1997	After winning a franchise-record 64 games in the regular season, the Jazz win the Western Conference title. They lose to the Chicago Bulls, four games to two, in the NBA Finals.

1998	Utah wins 62 regular-season games and a second straight Western Conference title. Again, they lose to the Bulls, four games to two, in the NBA Finals.
2003	Point guard Stockton ends his 19-year career, retiring as the NBA's all-time leader in assists and steals.
2003	Hall of Fame power forward Malone leaves the Jazz after 18 seasons. He signs with the Los Angeles Lakers and plays one more season.
2004	The Jazz miss the playoffs, ending a streak of 20 straight playoff appearances from 1984 to 2003.
2005	The Jazz select point guard Deron Williams with the third pick in the NBA Draft.
2007	Behind Williams, the Jazz win 51 games and reach the Western Conference finals before losing to the San Antonio Spurs.
2009	Former star Stockton and current coach Sloan are inducted into the Naismith Memorial Basketball Hall of Fame.
2010	Former star Malone is inducted into the Naismith Memorial Basketball Hall of Fame.
2011	In February, Sloan retires as Jazz coach after 23 seasons. Just days later, the team trades star point guard Williams to the New Jersey Nets.

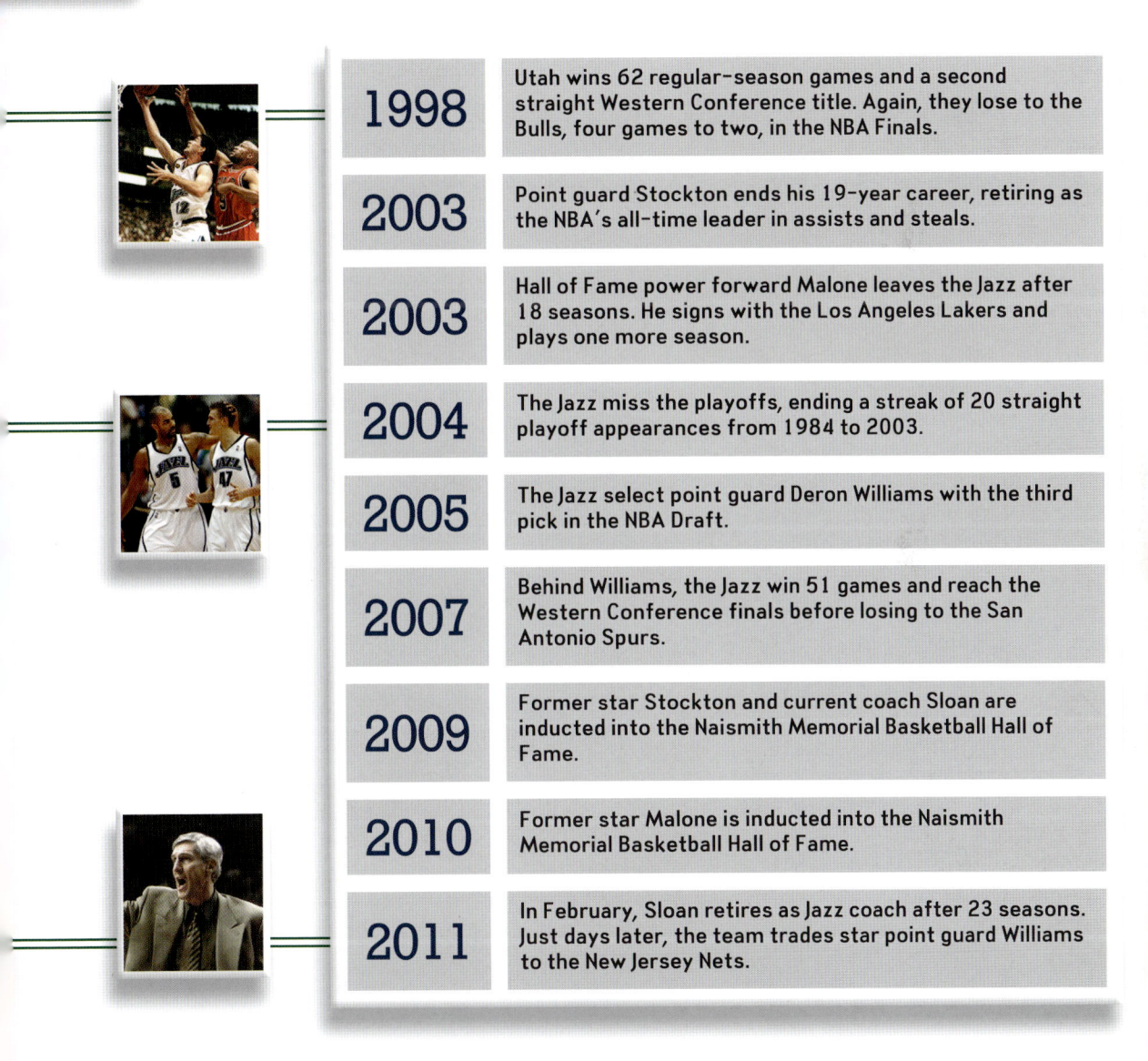

QUICK STATS

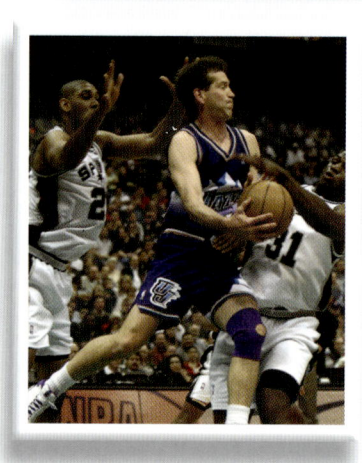

FRANCHISE HISTORY
New Orleans Jazz (1974–79)
Utah Jazz (1979–)

NBA FINALS
(wins in bold)
1997, 1998

CONFERENCE FINALS
1992, 1994, 1996, 1997, 1998, 2007

DIVISION CHAMPIONSHIPS
1984, 1989, 1992, 1997, 1998, 2000, 2007, 2008

KEY PLAYERS
(position[s]; seasons with team)
Thurl Bailey (F-C; 1983–92; 1999)
Carlos Boozer (F; 2004–10)
Adrian Dantley (F-G; 1979–86)
Mark Eaton (C; 1982–93)
Rickey Green (G; 1980–88)
Darrell Griffith (G; 1980–85, 1986–91)
Jeff Hornacek (G; 1993–2000)
Andrei Kirilenko (F; 2001–)
Karl Malone (F; 1985–2003)
Pete Maravich (G; 1974–80)
John Stockton (G; 1984–2003)
Deron Williams (G; 2005–2011)

KEY COACHES
Frank Layden (1981–88):
    277–294; 18–23 (postseason)
Jerry Sloan (1988–2011):
    1,127–682; 96–100 (postseason)

HOME ARENAS
Loyola Field House (1974–75)
Municipal Auditorium (1974–75)
Louisiana Superdome (1975–79)
Salt Palace (1979–91)
Delta Center/EnergySolutions Arena (1991–)

* All statistics through 2010–11 season

QUOTES AND ANECDOTES

When the Utah Jazz traded for 25-year-old Terry Furlow in 1980, they had visions of him being a big part of their rebuilding. That season, Furlow played well and averaged 16 points per game. That would be Furlow's only season in Utah, however. After the season, he was killed in an automobile accident.

As a kid in Louisiana, Karl Malone used to tell his mother, Shirley, "Mama, I'm going to own me a big truck someday." When he got to the NBA and could afford it, he bought an 18-wheel rig and often drove it. "Basketball is my job, but this is my love," he said.

For 18 years, John Stockton and Karl Malone were one of the great 1–2 punches in NBA history. "Stockton to Malone" became a familiar phrase for NBA fans. Both players are retired, but their connection has not ended. The former All-Stars are co-owners of a car dealership in the Salt Lake City area. The name of the dealership is, not surprisingly, Stockton to Malone Honda.

In 2009, John Stockton was inducted into the Naismith Memorial Basketball Hall of Fame. As part of his speech, he said, "To all the people who touched my life, helped me along, and brought out the best in me by whatever means, I'm overwhelmed and, yes, humbled. I can't begin to adequately thank even a few. I feel honored to stand up here in front of you and represent you on this stage tonight." Karl Malone was inducted into the Naismith Memorial Basketball Hall of Fame in 2010. In his speech, he said, "I hope I did it the way my peers did it before me. I didn't do anything but try to play hard."

GLOSSARY

assist

A pass that leads directly to a made basket.

contract

A binding agreement about, for example, years of commitment by a basketball player in exchange for a given salary.

draft

A system used by professional sports leagues to select new players in order to spread incoming talent among all teams. The NBA Draft is held each June.

franchise

An entire sports organization, including the players, coaches, and staff.

general manager

The executive who is in charge of the team's overall operation. He or she hires and fires coaches, drafts players, and signs free agents.

overtime

A period in a basketball game that is played to determine a winner when the four quarters end in a tie.

postseason

The games in which the best teams play after the regular-season schedule has been completed.

rebound

To secure the basketball after a missed shot.

rookie

A first-year player in the NBA.

roster

The players as a whole on a basketball team.

veteran

An individual with great experience in a particular endeavor.

FOR MORE INFORMATION

Further Reading

Ballard, Chris. *The Art of a Beautiful Game: The Thinking Fan's Tour of the NBA.* New York: Simon & Schuster, 2009.

Lazenby, Roland. *Stockton to Malone: The Rise of the Utah Jazz.* Lenexa, KS: Addax, 2002.

Simmons, Bill. *The Book of Basketball: The NBA According to the Sports Guy.* New York: Random House, 2009.

Web Links

To learn more about the Utah Jazz, visit ABDO Publishing Company online at **www.abdopublishing.com**. Web sites about the Jazz are featured on our Book Links page. These links are routinely monitored and updated to provide the most current information available.

Places To Visit

EnergySolutions Arena
301 West South Temple
Salt Lake City, UT 84101
801-325-2000
www.energysolutionsarena.com
Formerly known as the Delta Center, this has been the Jazz's home arena since the 1991–92 season.

Greater New Orleans Sports Hall of Fame
Louisiana Superdome
1500 Sugar Bowl Drive
New Orleans, LA 70112-1255
www.allstatesugarbowl.org/site64.php
This Hall of Fame honors New Orleans natives who have achieved prominence in sports or others who have achieved prominence in New Orleans.

Naismith Memorial Basketball Hall of Fame
1000 West Columbus Avenue
Springfield, MA 01105
413-781-6500
www.hoophall.com
This hall of fame and museum highlights the greatest players and moments in the history of basketball. Adrian Dantley, Karl Malone, Pete Maravich, John Stockton, and coach Jerry Sloan are among the former Jazz players enshrined.

47

INDEX

Atlanta Hawks, 16, 25

Bailey, Thurl, 25, 28, 30
Battistone, Sam (owner), 15, 21
Boone, Ron, 22
Boozer, Carlos, 38, 39, 40
Boston Celtics, 22
Bristow, Allan, 22
Buffalo Braves, 23

Chicago Bulls, 10–12, 34, 39, 40

Dantley, Adrian, 22–25, 28, 29–30
Delta Center, 11
Denver Nuggets, 28, 37
Detroit Pistons, 18, 24, 30
Dream Team, 7
Drew, John, 25, 28, 30

Eaton, Mark, 25, 28, 31

Favors, Derrick, 40

Goodrich, Gail, 18–19
Green, Rickey, 25, 28, 30, 31
Griffith, Darrell, 25, 27, 28, 31

Harris, Devin, 40
Hornacek, Jeff, 9, 12, 33
Houston Rockets, 10, 33, 34

Indiana Pacers, 23

Jefferson, Al, 40

Kirilenko, Andrei, 38, 41

Layden, Frank (general manager and coach), 22–25, 27, 28–30, 31–32
Los Angeles Lakers, 10, 18, 23, 37
Louisiana Jazz, 12, 15–19, 22
Louisiana Superdome, 17–18
Loyola Field House, 17

Malone, Karl, 5–12, 30, 32, 33, 37–38, 39, 41
Maravich, "Pistol Pete," 16–17, 18–19, 22
Millsap, Paul, 41
Moore, Otto, 18
Municipal Auditorium, 17

NBA Finals
 1997, 9–10, 34
 1998, 10–12, 34
New Jersey Nets, 40
Nissalke, Tom (coach), 25

Okur, Mehmet, 38
Ostertag, Greg, 9

Phoenix Suns, 18, 28

Robertson, Scotty (coach), 17
Robinson, Len "Truck," 18
Rosenfeld, Fred (owner), 15
Russell, Bryon, 9

Salt Palace, 22
San Antonio Spurs, 10, 33, 39, 40
Sloan, Jerry (coach), 6, 9, 10, 32–33, 38, 40, 41
Stockton, John, 5–12, 30, 33, 34, 37–38, 41

Tripucka, Kelly, 30

Utah Stars, 21–22

Van Breda Kolff, Bill (coach), 17

Wilkins, Dominique, 25
Williams, Deron, 38, 39–40, 41
Williams, Freeman, 25

About the Author

Brian Howell is a freelance writer based in Denver, Colorado. He has written several books for young readers. Howell has been a sports journalist for more than 17 years, writing about high school, college, and professional athletics, including covering major sporting events such as the US Open golf tournament, the World Series, the Stanley Cup playoffs, the NBA All-Star Game, and the NBA playoffs. He has earned several writing awards during his career.